PICTURESQUE
LAKE DISTRICT

A PHOTOGRAPHIC SOUVENIR IN BEAUTIFUL COLOUR

SALMON

The dramatic slope of Langdale Fell rises steeply from the valley floor of the Great Langdale Valley. From the vantage point of Wrynose Fell, the isolated farmsteads and fields with their drystone walls take on a toy-like scale dwarfed by the massive peaks on all sides.

Reflected in the tranquil waters of Blea Tarn, the distinctive peaks of the Langdale Pikes rise to 2,300 feet. Dominating the landscape around the head of Windermere they are frequently photographed and painted and it is one of the most popular area for walks.

Enclosed by steep fells with attractive woodlands growing beside the shore, Grasmere is one of the prettiest of all the lakes. Rowing-boats are a popular way to explore the lake and are the only means of visiting the solitary island that lies at its heart.

A small sheet of water almost encircled by trees, Loughrigg Tarn lies to the north of Skelwith Bridge beneath the slopes of Loughrigg Fell.
An easy footpath can be followed along the shoreline and in autumn the rich colours create an especially spectacular scene.

On a still winter's day it is clear why Derwentwater has a reputation as one of the most beautiful of the lakes. Cat Bells rises from the far shore of the lake, at the foot of which lies Brandelhow Park, the first property to be purchased in the area by The National Trust.

The quaint 17th century Old Bridge House straddles the little Stock Ghyll in the ancient market town of Ambleside, a popular Lakeland centre. Originally built as a summer-house for Ambleside Hall, it is now owned by The National Trust and used as an information centre.

Like many of the western lakes, Crummock Water, with its indented shoreline and wooded slopes, is surrounded by wild and romantic scenery. At one time it was joined to nearby Buttermere and today they are only separated by a narrow strip of land.

The isolated church of St. Bartholomew overlooks pretty Loweswater, one of the westernmost of the lakes. Originating as a small chapel, the church was much enlarged in the late 19th century to meet the needs of the local mining community.

Charming 17th century Hill Top Farm near Hawkshead was once the home of Beatrix Potter, well-known author of *Peter Rabbit* and many other nursery classics. Now maintained by The National Trust it is a place of pilgrimage for thousands of visitors.

Standing near the head of Esthwaite Water, the village of Hawkshead has many quaint old corners where cottages cluster around secluded courtyards. The sturdy Parish Church of St. Michael stands above the village overlooking the Esthwaite Valley.

One of the northern lakes, Ullswater is often busy with yachts and other pleasure craft, and passenger steamers also provide a pleasant way to explore the lake. The head of Ullswater is surrounded by some of the Lake District's most impressive scenery.

A traditional boat-house stands reflected in the waters of Ullswater at Pooley Bridge. Iron Age remains can be found on the surrounding
hills and the village is a popular centre for many outdoor activities including pony-trekking, fishing, sailing, as well as walking.

The most popular centre for visitors to Windermere, Bowness-on-Windermere always presents a busy scene in the summer months. The first public steamer service on Windermere was launched in 1845 and there is still a regular service to Ambleside and Lakeside.

Over five miles long, Coniston Water has wooded banks and is dotted with pretty little islands. The dramatic setting for several water-speed record attempts, the western shore of the lake is dominated by the distinctive shape of the 2,635 feet high The Old Man of Coniston.

Lying to the south-east of Derwentwater, Watendlath is a remote little valley. The small hamlet of Watendlath consists mainly of farmhouses which are now owned by The National Trust, and the small beck is crossed here by an ancient pack-horse bridge.

One of the smaller lakes, Buttermere is nonetheless one of the most spectacular. Standing 250 feet above sea-level, it is ringed on three sides by steep mountains including the impressive bulk of Fleetwith Pike and the distinctive ridge known as Haystacks.

An evocative structure whose original function has become lost in the mists of time, Castlerigg Stone Circle stands on a hill to the east of Keswick. Said to date from around 1400 BC, it consists of some forty stones in a large circle with a smaller group within it.

One of the most photographed and painted scenes in the Lake District, the view of Derwentwater from Ashness Bridge is spectacular in all seasons. The little bridge is probably early 18th century and was built for the pack-horses which were the only means of transport.

Waterhead stands at the north-east corner of Windermere adjoining Ambleside. It is one of the ports of call for the steamers which ply the lake and is a busy centre for boating activities of all kinds with rowing-boats and motor day boats available for hire from the landings.

Typical of the area, Jesus Church stands in the village of Troutbeck, some two miles to the north of Windermere. In Roman times the slopes of the Troutbeck Valley would have been thickly wooded, but centuries of farming have left it a pleasing patchwork of fields.

The Lake District has close associations with many writers and poets, but perhaps the closest is with William Wordsworth. He lived in the village of Rydal for many years and is responsible for the mass of daffodils in Dora's Field, named after his daughter.

The largest of the lakes and the most popular for water sports, Windermere lies in a valley formed by glaciers in the last Ice Age. Seen here from the slopes of Brant Fell, at its northern end it is bordered by wooded slopes and lush fields of grazing sheep and cattle.

The inspiring mass of Scafell towers above the waters of Wastwater, the deepest of the lakes plunging to a depth of 268 feet. Scafell is one of only a handful of English mountains higher than 3,000 feet and in the winter it is usually capped with a blanketing of snow.

Dominating the scene near the hamlet of Wasdale Head is Great Gable, one of the highest peaks in the Lake District. Chosen as the emblem of the Lake District National Park, the view of the mountain across the waters of Wastwater is the epitome of Lakeland scenery.

The prosperous and attractive town of Kendal is the main southern gateway to the Lake District. Situated amongst more gentle countryside, it was granted its charter for a market in 1189 and the ruined Norman castle was the birthplace of Katherine Parr, last wife of Henry VIII.

Standing on the shore of Derwentwater, Keswick is an attractive old market town with narrow streets and sturdy grey stone buildings.
Rowing-boats lie drawn up at the boat landings with the distinctive shapes of Causey Pike and Cat Bells rising beyond the lake.

The road from Ambleside to Coniston passes through the hamlet of Skelwith Bridge in the beautiful Brathay Valley. Close by, is this impressive waterfall where the River Brathay and Langdale Beck come together and tumble over a sixteen feet drop.

Picturesque Dove Cottage in the village of Grasmere was home to William Wordsworth and his sister Dorothy for nine years and it was here that he brought his bride after their marriage in 1802. Many of his finest poems were composed here and it is maintained as a museum to his life.

Between Hawkshead and Yewdale, some two miles north-east of Coniston, is the open wilderness of Tarn Hows. At one time there were three smaller lakes until the building of a dam created the larger one that we see today and it is considered one of the prettiest of the lakes.

The main road from Patterdale to Ambleside is carried over the Kirkstone Pass, a wild and desolate area between Red Screes and Caudale Moor. It is the highest pass in the region open to motorists, reaching 1,489 feet, and from the summit there are magnificent views.

The area around Ullswater was always greatly admired by William Wordsworth. His famous poem, *The Daffodils*, was inspired by the sight of wild daffodils growing in profusion at Gowbarrow Park on the northern shore of the lake and they are still a colourful sight in spring.

Aira Force is a spectacular waterfall near Gowbarrow Fell on the northern side of Ullswater. It plunges down in one almost sheer drop
over a 60 foot high rocky precipice and is crossed by bridges which give dramatic views of the gorge and the surrounding scenery.

Enfolded in beautiful countryside between Ambleside and Grasmere, Rydal Water is the smallest sheet of water in the Lake District to be designated as a lake. It is owned by The National Trust who prohibit private boats, thus preserving the lake's peace and tranquillity.

Near the town of Keswick is the rocky, pine-clad promontory of Friar's Crag jutting out into the waters of Derwentwater. It takes its name from the monks who, in the 7th century, were reputed to have embarked to visit St. Herbert at his hermitage on an island.

Stretching for nearly four miles, Thirlmere was created at the end of the 19th century when the valley was flooded to create a reservoir.
A popular area with walkers, there are many footpaths and trails through the coniferous woodland that borders the lake.